I can draw
Magical Creatures

DK

LONDON, NEW YORK, MUNICH, MELBOURNE, and DELHI

DESIGNED BY Penny Lamprell & Laura Roberts-Jensen
ILLUSTRATED BY Clare Wilson & the Peter Bull Art Studio
WRITTEN AND EDITED BY Carrie Love & Lorrie Mack
US EDITOR Margaret Parrish
PHOTOGRAPHY BY Andy Crawford
PUBLISHING MANAGER Susan Leonard
PRODUCTION Seyhan Esen-Yagmurlu
JACKET DESIGNER Karen Hood
DTP DESIGNER Almudena Díaz
CONSULTANT Emma Drew

First American Edition, 2006
Published in the United States by
DK Publishing, Inc., 375 Hudson Street
New York, New York 10014

06 07 08 09 10 10 9 8 7 6 5 4 3 2 1

Copyright © 2006 Dorling Kindersley Limited

A Cataloging-in-Publication record for this book is available from the Library of Congress.

ISBN-13 978-0-7566-1986-2
ISBN-10 0-7566-1986-6

Color reproduction by ICON, United Kingdom
Printed and bound in Slovakia by Tlaciarne BB S.R.O.

Discover more at
www.dk.com

Contents

Useful stuff

CREATE YOUR OWN MAGIC with the tools below. Bring your drawings to life with colors and shading.

Oil pastels for coloring in your drawings.

Soft pastels can create a gentle look which is good for fairies and princesses.

No. 2 pencil

4B soft pencil

charcoal

For shading effects, use an eraser or your finger to smudge soft pastels and charcoal.

colored paper

sketch pad

colored pencils

pencil sharpener

Color in a drawing with water-soluble colored pencils. Use a wet paintbrush to soften the color and make it look more like paint.

References

Stuck for ideas? Take a look around you and see what inspiration you can get from toys, magazines, and newspapers.

feathers

pictures from magazines, postcards, and books

felt-tip pen for strong color

ballpoint pen for strong outlines

toy figures and puppets for reference

jewels

1 Use a large oval for the fairy's head, and smaller circles for her joints, hands, and feet. Lines make up her arms and legs.

2 Give the fairy wings and a wand. Draw in her hands, arms, and legs.

Flower fairy

I AM A FLOWER FAIRY, see how I flutter my wings. I am as pretty as a petal. I sprinkle magical fairy dust with my wand.

3 Add eyes, hair, a mouth, and a nose. Decorate your fairy with a pretty dress and striped stockings.

Use shading to decorate your fairy's dress.

1 Start with some circles and lines.

2 Draw arms, hands, wings, feet, and legs.

3 Draw in your ballerina's face, hair, and dress.

Ballerina fairy

HERE IS THE LOVELY dancing fairy, so light on her toes. Make her dance around your page.

1 Use lines as the basis of your fairy's arms and legs. Circle and oval shapes make up the feet, hands, and head.

2 Give your fairy wings, legs, arms, a hand, and a tooth to hold.

3 Draw hair, eyes, a nose, and a mouth. Give your fairy a pretty dress to wear.

Use shading and stippling to decorate your fairy's hair and dress.

Tooth fairy

Zzzzz

DREAM OF TWINKLY STARS, as your very own Tooth fairy comes to swap your tooth for some money!

taddaaaa!

Fairy faces

YOUR PENCILS, PENS, AND PASTELS are like magic wands. Use them to make your fairies look beautiful!

Try some smaller flowers for your fairy's crown.

Fairy headwear

There are plenty of ways to dress up your fairies. Create amazing headwear for them to fly around in.

Here's an interesting design!

Make a pretty hat that looks like one big flower.

This fairy's hairstyle
is fun and easy to draw.

Fairy hairstyles

Be creative with your drawings and
give your fairies some fun hairdos.
You're the one with the pencil so you
can decide what to try out; short
and curly or long and wavy!

Decorate your
fairy's hair
with a ribbon
and give her
a necklace
to wear.

Draw thick and
wavy hair using
curved lines and
shading.

To get this
unusual
hairstyle use
lots of
spirals in a
pile on top of
her head.

Fairytastic

13

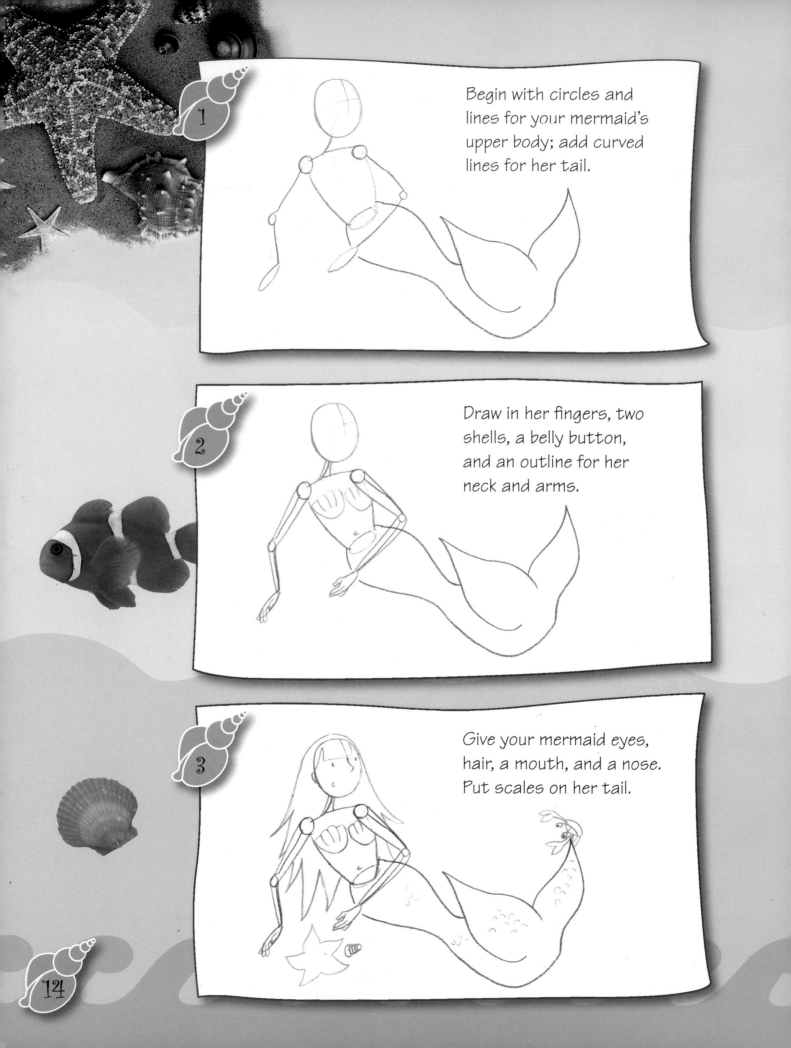

1 Begin with circles and lines for your mermaid's upper body; add curved lines for her tail.

2 Draw in her fingers, two shells, a belly button, and an outline for her neck and arms.

3 Give your mermaid eyes, hair, a mouth, and a nose. Put scales on her tail.

Mermaid

"I LOVE TO SPLASH AROUND IN THE WAVES and I swim with the fish. I visit the shore every now and then, but I live in the sea since I can't stay out of the water for too long!"

Magical colors

H AVE FUN AND GET CREATIVE when coloring in your magical creatures. See the amazing difference that pastels, water-soluble colored pencils, and felt-tip pens can make!

Witch

Color in your witch's hair, dress, and shoes with colored pencils. Don't make her dress a solid black; use shading to make it lighter in some areas. Create a rough texture on her hair and broomstick using oil pastels.

Wizard

Using felt-tip pens, make your wizard's cloak look like velvet. He is a wise and old wizard so keep his hair and beard white.

Flower Fairy

This flower fairy has been colored in with soft pastels. Use two colors and blend them together.

Before you get going try out some different combinations of colors and materials on the side of the page.

Mermaid

Color in your pretty mermaid with water-soluble colored pencils.

Elf

Use colored pencils to decorate your elf. Try different shades of green for his hat and shirt. Add depth to your drawing by shading his bag and scarf to make them look worn.

Princess

MEET THE PRETTY PRINCESS. She looks sweet in her patterned dress. She lives in a magical kingdom. If she kisses the frog he might turn into a prince!

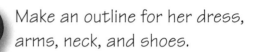
ribbit!

1 — Begin with basic shapes and lines for your drawing.

2 — Make an outline for her dress, arms, neck, and shoes.

Use shading and coloring to dress up your princess!

3 Draw her hair, eyes, mouth and nose. Add a crown, hearts on her dress, and a frog for her to hold.

1 Basic shapes and lines make up the main body parts for the prince.

2 Draw an outline around the prince's body. Give him a cloak and clothes.

Prince

Draw a royal prince who is ready to rule a kingdom, fight a dragon, and charm a princess. In order to look the part he needs a crown, a sword, and a stylish cloak.

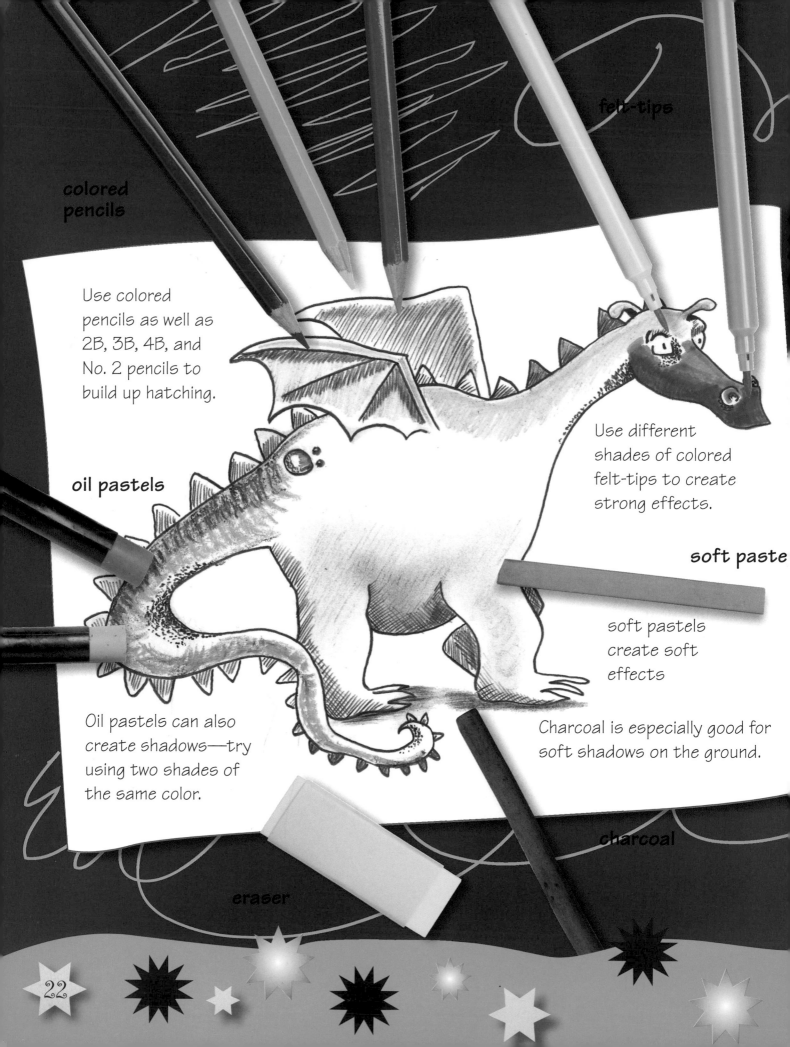

colored
pencils

felt-tips

Use colored
pencils as well as
2B, 3B, 4B, and
No. 2 pencils to
build up hatching.

oil pastels

Use different
shades of colored
felt-tips to create
strong effects.

soft paste

soft pastels
create soft
effects

Oil pastels can also
create shadows—try
using two shades of
the same color.

Charcoal is especially good for
soft shadows on the ground.

eraser

charcoal

22

Types of shading

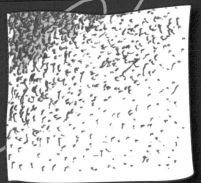

Soft, diagonal lines will add depth to your drawing, but make sure not to press too hard.

When crosshatching, draw lines in two directions, one over the other, pressing lightly.

In stippling, shading is created by using lots of tiny dots.

Shading

He looks a bit shady...

CREATE A 3-D EFFECT on your drawings with clever shading. Make your dragons and witches look more scary, and your princess and prince more important by using areas of light and dark.

Shady wings

See how these wings have been improved with dark and light shading.

1 Start with cirles in different sizes for the unicorn's head, body, and leg joints.

2 Draw an outline for the body. Give it a tail, ears, and a horn. Draw two curved lines for its wings.

3 Finish the wing with lots of curved lines in a row. Give the unicorn a mane, eyes, a mouth, and nose. Decorate its horn.

Unicorn

A UNICORN IS A MYTHICAL CREATURE with magical powers. It looks like a horse, but one with wings and a horn coming out of its forehead.

Use shading to make your drawing look more interesting.

1 Draw straight lines for the neck and legs, a squiggly line for the tail, and circles for the head and main body.

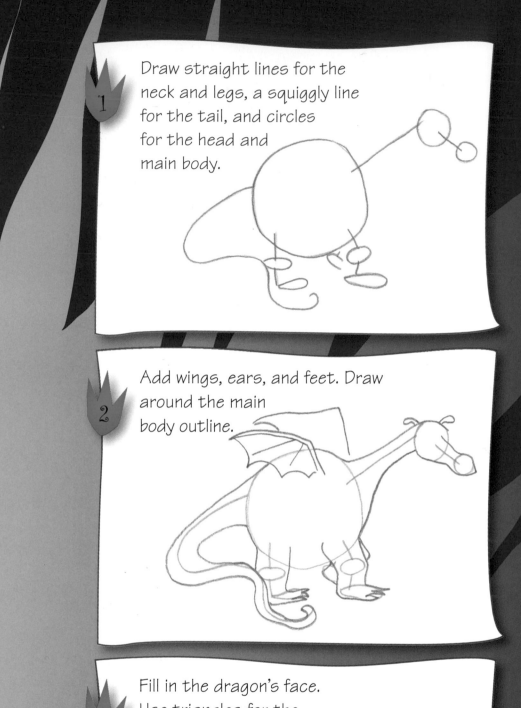

2 Add wings, ears, and feet. Draw around the main body outline.

3 Fill in the dragon's face. Use triangles for the ridges on his back.

Dragon

LEGENDS FROM DIFFERENT COUNTRIES describe dragons as large fire-breathing reptiles with wings. Dragons were seen as terrifying creatures that often guarded treasure or maidens.

Puff!

Use shading on the dragon's body to make him look more lifelike.

1 Draw circles, semicircles, squiggly lines, and a triangle.

2 Create an outline around the dragon's body, head, and tail. Give him wings!

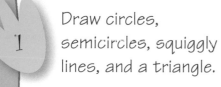

1 Begin with basic shapes and curved lines.

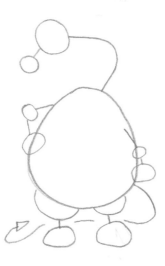

2 Draw around the shapes to make your dragon.

Draw eyes, a mouth, and nose. Use shading on his wings.

More dragons

I N FAIRY TALES PEOPLE were terrified of dragons because they were thought to fly and breathe fire. Princes were sent off to kill dragons in order to protect people— and rescue princesses.

Use shading on his skin and draw lines on the front of his belly and neck.

1 Draw a large circle for the elf's head, and lines for his legs and arms. Use basic shapes for his body, feet, and joints.

2 Give your elf shorts and a T-shirt to wear. Draw an outline around his arms, hands, and legs.

Elf

ELVES ARE A TYPE OF FAIRY that are popular in myths. These tiny people are said to be friendly to humans, although sometimes they can misbehave! Santa Claus has elves working for him as his helpers.

3 Add in his eyes, mouth, ears, and nose. Draw a hat and a bag. Dress him in striped tights and shoes.

Use shading on your elf's tights, scarf, and bag.

31

Elf parade

Have fun drawing the elves on their parade. Do you think they are on their way to Santa's workshop?

Once you've drawn some elves try drawing lots of trees and snow!

Bearded elf

Friendly elves

Begin with basic shapes and lines, then give clothes, shoes, and bags to the elves.

1

2

Copy the shapes and lines in step 1. Draw an outline for the elf's body.

1

2

Friendly elf

Draw me a hat!

Use different colors and shading techniques to decorate your drawings.

Helpful elf

Follow the circles and lines in step 1, then give your drawing more details.

Start with shapes and lines, then give the elf a big nose, clothes, and an apple to hold.

1

2

1

2

1 Start with basic shapes for the main parts of the wizard's body and lines for his legs, arms, and neck.

2 Draw a hat and a magical wand. Dress your wizard in a long gown.

Wizard

WATCH THE WIZARD as he waves his star-shaped wand to perform magical spells and tricks. He is powerful and his name means "wise man." The most famous wizard was named Merlin. Have you heard of him?

Give him some hair and a beard. Fill in his face with big eyebrows, a nose, and mouth.

3

Abracadabra

Decorate his gown with yellow stars and moons. Use shading on his hat and gown to make them look real.

Expressions

"MIRROR, MIRROR, ON THE WALL, who is the fairest of them all?" Try drawing different expressions on your magical creatures' faces.

Sad fairy

Draw the fairy's head, neck, and eyes.

Add a nose, mouth, and teardrops.

Give her wings, hair, and a crown.

Happy witch

Draw the witch's head, neck, shoulders, and eyes.

Draw her nose with a wart, her hair, mouth, and chin.

Shade in her hair and draw a hat.

Angry goblin

Use two crossed lines to draw eyes in the right place.

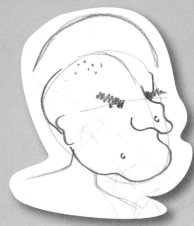

Draw his jawline, eyebrows, nose, and an ear.

Draw his hair and shade it in. Put stubble on his chin.

Tired giant

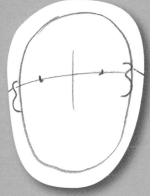

Draw the giant's head, eyes, and ears.

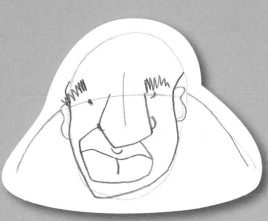

Put in detail on his face and give him shoulders.

Shade in his lips and hair.

Surprised elf

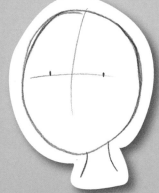

Start by drawing the elf's head, neck, and eyes.

Add a nose, mouth, ears, and eyebrows.

Draw a hat and shade in his eyebrows and mouth.

Start with circles and basic shapes for the witch's body and broom.

Give your witch a hat, arms, hands, and cloak. Draw a cat sitting on her broom.

Draw a nose, mouth, and eyes on the witch and her cat. Give the witch some hair.

Witch

Hubble bubble, here comes trouble... watch out for the flying witch and her cat. Stay away from her cauldron!

1 Begin with basic lines and shapes for the giant's head, body, legs, and arms.

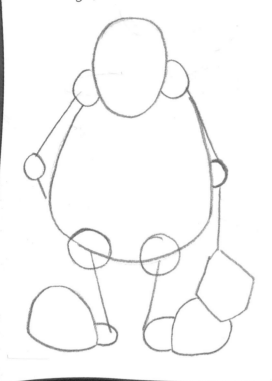

2 Draw around the shapes and lines to create the arms, body, fingers, and legs.

Giant

"FEE, FI, FO, FUM! I smell the blood of an Englishman. You had better stay away from my hen that lays solid-gold eggs, or I won't be a happy, friendly giant!"

Texture

MAGICAL CREATURES have a range of textures, from feathery wings on fairies to shiny scales on dragons. Try out different materials to make your magical creatures look lifelike.

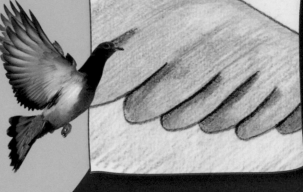

Wings need long, soft pencil strokes to make the feathers soft and light.

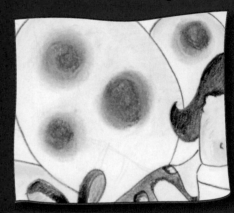

Use a soft pencil or pastel to make fairy wings look light and delicate.

Words to think about

scaly furry **bumpy**

lumpy **smooth** slimy

hairy prickly spiky

feathery **shiny**

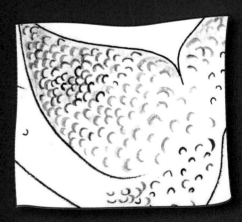

Mermaid tails and bodies have overlapping scales that have a texture like fish skin.

Textures in nature

Look around you (in your home, outside, and in books) to get ideas for adding more texture to your drawings. Can you guess where each texture is from?

This flowery texture would make a delicate fairy wing.

Ssscales are ssso sssuper

Look at these shimmery scales.

A unicorn could fly away with these feathers.

These lumps and bumps are like a witch's warty nose.

Dragons' wings can stretch like this.

Copy this texture to create a fairy's fluttery wings.

Could this be a dragon's scaly skin?

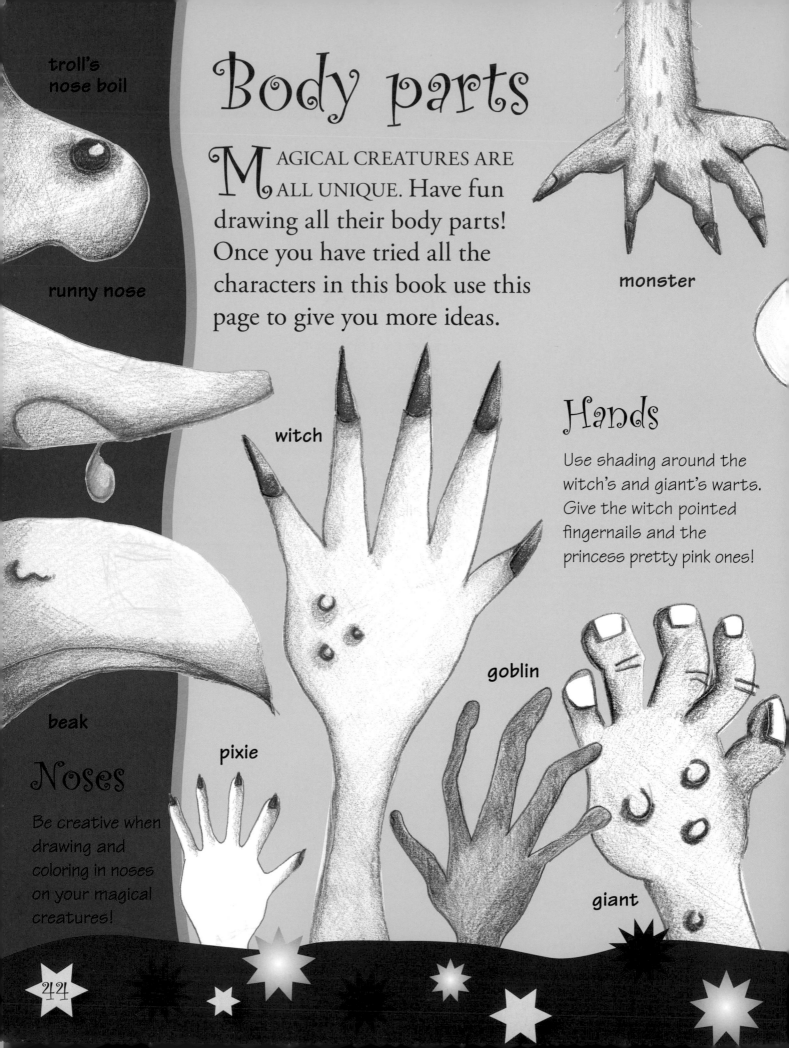

troll's nose boil

runny nose

beak

Noses

Be creative when drawing and coloring in noses on your magical creatures!

Body parts

MAGICAL CREATURES ARE ALL UNIQUE. Have fun drawing all their body parts! Once you have tried all the characters in this book use this page to give you more ideas.

monster

witch

Hands

Use shading around the witch's and giant's warts. Give the witch pointed fingernails and the princess pretty pink ones!

goblin

pixie

giant

44

troll

gnome

dragon

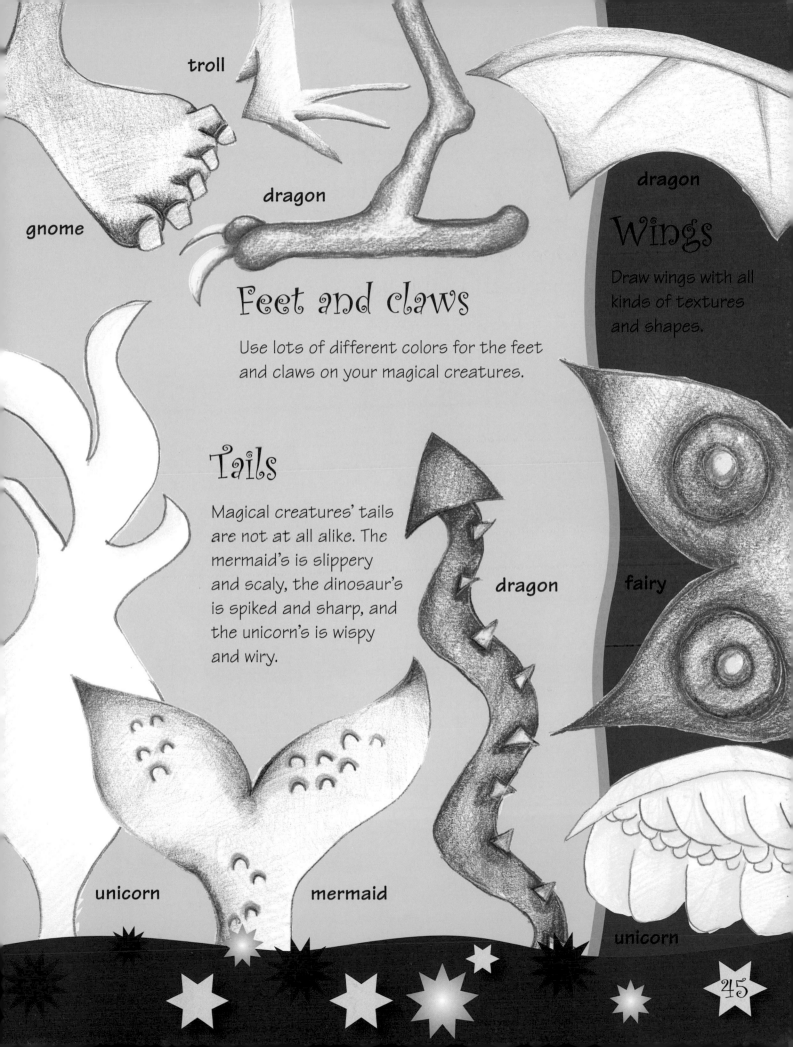

dragon

Wings

Draw wings with all kinds of textures and shapes.

Feet and claws

Use lots of different colors for the feet and claws on your magical creatures.

Tails

Magical creatures' tails are not at all alike. The mermaid's is slippery and scaly, the dinosaur's is spiked and sharp, and the unicorn's is wispy and wiry.

dragon

fairy

unicorn

mermaid

unicorn

Scale

MAGICAL CREATURES are very different in size. There are tiny fairies and gigantic giants. Be creative and try drawing a few magical creatures on one page. Make sure you keep them to scale.

We're only little

Tiny fairies

Fairies are usually very small. Have fun comparing your drawings to real-life objects to see the difference in size.

Fee fi fo fum?

Silly sizes

You can play around by changing the scale of different creatures around to make some funny pictures. This giant isn't so big now that he's standing by an oversized elf!

Hmmm... I think I prefer the frog

Life-size

Some magical creatures should be drawn to look life-size, such as the prince, princess, and unicorn.

Fly away

The witch looks like she is farther away because she is smaller than the flying dragon.

Any size

Some magical creatures come in many shapes and sizes. Dragons can be big and scary or small and sweet. Try drawing both!

Where's the beach?

Index

It's magical.
Bye bye!

Acknowledgments

Dorling Kindersley would like to thank: Karen Hood, Tory Gordon-Harris, and Jane Bull for design inspiration; Rose Horridge and Claire Bowers for picture research; Zahavit Shalev and Fleur Star for editorial assistance.

Picture credits

Picture credits t = top b = bottom c= center l = left r = right

© Judith Miller / Dorling Kindersley / The Design Gallery 36tr.